Haiku

Published by Ponty Press

Special thanks to Eve Phoebe Lewis, Moira Andrew, Sally Spedding, Mike Jenkins, Jolen Whitworth, Ferris Gilli, Sue Gurman, Sandy, Lili, my passport and the world around me

ISBN: 978-1-4716-7700-7

Front cover design and illustrations: Dave Lewis
Back cover photograph: Dave Jones

By the same author:
Layer Cake © 2009
Urban Birdsong © 2010
Sawing Fallen Logs For Ladybird Houses © 2011
Ctrl-Alt-Delete © 2011

Edited:
Welsh Poetry Competition Anthology © 2011

Website: www.david-lewis.co.uk

Dave Lewis

Haiku

'A collection of mostly modern moments'

For Eve

the sparrow hops
along the veranda
with wet feet
- *Issa*

CONTENTS

Introduction

Haiku is a small poetical form, usually but not always of three short lines, that attempts to juxtapose two images or ideas. The separation of the elements creates a sensation or emotion in the reader. A haiku captures a 'moment' in time, perhaps a mood, or a sound, a smell or a taste and forms a complete living entity. A good haiku, like any good poem, is distilled and paints a vivid picture which the reader must complete.

Haiku originated in 17th Century Japan and seems to have evolved from the earlier 14th Century 'Renga' (literally: linked songs) – a collaborative form with strict guidelines and great length. Haiku as we know it today derives from the opening verse of renga.

Many early Japanese poets were monks or teachers and one of the most famous of these was Basho (1644-1694), who was a Zen Buddhist. This is important when we look at the make-up of a traditional haiku. We get the moment of instant perception and simplicity from Buddhism whilst the Zen brings us a de-emphasizing of knowledge in favour of

1

direct self-realization. Thus haiku can be viewed as a 'mind set' or 'spiritual way'.

After losing its way slightly haiku was made accessible to wider audiences again by the great poet Issa (1763-1827), whose unhappy childhood and hugely tragic life is present in much of his poetry.

Other writers, like Shiki (1867-1902), modernized haiku as they disliked much of the current trends in Japanese literature and were heavily influenced by Western culture. He created a style of haiku known as 'sketching from life' and it was Shiki who is credited with separating the first stanza of a renga and allowing it to stand alone as a haiku.

The mid-20th Century saw writers like Blyth and Henderson seeking to translate Japanese haiku and make it more accessible to the West while imagists like Ezra Pound (1885-1972) stressed the importance of brevity, directness and music in all poetry.

Pound felt that an image should avoid parable and even metaphor, and be capable of being grasped instantly. His famous 'metro station' piece became a precursor for modern day urban haiku, where topics such as cars, buildings, computers and shopping centres are all fashionable subject matter nowadays.

In the 1950s the beat generation of poets became endeared and liberated by haiku. Jack Kerouac (1922-1969) often put haiku in letters and in the middle of novels as a means of pinpointing a particular moment in time and place.

Alan Ginsberg published haiku throughout his long career, and in 2004, at the age of 74, Gary Snyder was awarded The Masaoka Shiki International Haiku Grand Prize for his contribution to the art of haiku internationally.

Today there seems to be almost two schools of thought:

The stricter and more traditional approach, in English, is to use three or less lines with 17 syllables, add in a seasonal word (or kigo) and a cut (sometimes indicated by a punctuation mark) to highlight where the reader needs to contrast and compare two images.

To use the present tense of the verb in order to preserve 'the moment' is encouraged as well as obeying several other rules like avoiding simile, metaphor or personification.

However, in modern society where many of us are pushed further away from the natural world, haiku, like all poetry, has evolved to become ever more urban based and so I believe it is therefore important to have a broader approach to haiku and to reflect these new sources of inspiration. And today it is almost impossible to categorise any particular style, format, or subject matter as definitive.

Therefore in the more radical haiku a modern proponent may abandon the rules completely and instead of focusing on nature may illicit hi-tech gadgets, inner-city living, iPhones and technology in their writing as well as using a change of form, line break, punctuation, shape and length.

Kerouac himself wrote '...a haiku must be very simple and free of all poetic trickery...'.

But, there are single line haiku (monoku), two lines, four lines, 'vertical' and 'circular'. In fact almost anything goes as we see haiku evolution changing its focus and influence in our ever-changing 21st Century world.

4

As a result almost anyone can write and understand a haiku. And as a hard copy record of the precise instant of inspiration and experience there is no better form.

From my own personal viewpoint, whether in art, photography, poetry or music I believe all rules are meant to be broken and so with regards to haiku whilst I often revel in the moment and have a dislike for 'over-creating' for the sake of it I do concede there is room for a small degree of 'crafting the moment', maybe just tweaking that emotional outpouring to render it more lucid or universal.

For as the great haiku advocate Jane Reichhold says 'Perhaps, nothing is absolute in haiku. Like life, haiku require learning, experience and balance.'

Many haiku writers use the five elements of Taoism as the themes with which to organise their poems. The antagonistic yin and yang approach of using wood, fire, earth, metal and water links in well with the natural aspect of haiku where the energy of the cycle is either productive or destructive.

When thinking of some sort of structure for this particular collection though, I decided to use the four seasons as headings. I was amazed, but not surprised, to discover my writing adjusted with the changing time of year and also as I found myself becoming drawn more and more into the genre.

As for the quality of the haiku I will of course let the reader decide but rather than omit a few lesser poems I decided I could afford to be a little extravagant in order to fully record my own sense of time and place in this ever-changing environment we all find ourselves struggling to cope with. That said I'm sure I will continue to write haiku and in the years to come will hopefully have many more to share.

And finally, although not 100% convinced it was a good idea, having seen it in many haiku collections, I eventually decided to include at the end of this book some brief notes which may help to explain certain moments a little better.

Either way I hope you enjoy reading these poems as much as I enjoyed living them.

Dave Lewis
Spring 2012

Spring

St. David's Day –
  Eve has two daffodils
one for her doll

beneath the old oak
a party of bluebells
reckless birdsong

picking through staves
  of telephone lines –
musical birds

March buds open
  the moon is larger
Than a football

students of the East
  walking
through the green wood

The sound of lawnmowers –
  clouds march
across a blue sky

my princess
leaves her sand castles
to the rising tide

Dog on decking
  sniffing north
Spring arriving soon

A woman with a smile
  points out –
You have eyeliner

Dappled sunlight
  on the wooden floor
Water untouched in your dish

You looked at me
　and then the new moon
one last time

　　　　　Your toy rat
　　　　　　waits for you
　　　　　to kill him again

The house is quiet –
　no pitter-patters
on the wooden floor

　　　　　My cornflakes taste
　　　　　　of salt
　　　　　As I write

Monday morning saying
　'ta ra San…'
To an empty chair

Tears suddenly
  without warning
explode from my stomach

                    My muddy boots
                      are clean –
                    Running through the dew

Time ticks through
  an empty house
A robin hops along the decking

                    My jacket is free
                      of 'Bloody hair!'
                    Not my own

Pillows smell
  of lavender
Not dandelions

Eaten by next door's cat
  while looking for worms
The blackbird

Books unread
  bursting from the wall
Drunk –

Familiar hangover
  on a Sunday
Afternoon dragging

Washing blowing
  on the line –
sketching my future

travellers reading guidebooks
as the pilot chases dawn
on the edge of the world

Plopping frogs and lotus flowers
Waiting for the monks to finish prayers
Dambulla

       bowing elephant
       at the sacred relic of the tooth
       hot sun

dreams continue
after safari ends –
grey clouds rolling

       Smelling buds
        their perfume pointless
       Without you

Old newspapers
  on the carpet
I start work tomorrow

Bloated with memories
  pockmarked with guilt
Gathering bluebells in silence

                                        time
                    puts scars on scars
                    – brambles

Lilac bluebells
  under your watchful gaze
bloom

                    Sheep-empty meadow
                      you snap a twig
                    a blackbird rises

towering cliffs –
clinging for their lives
green trees

Horse mane on barbed wire
  a Rose in your hair
to disguise the thorns

           dawn breeze –
           woodsmoke threads
           the green forest

Continents of puddles
  the world traveller
in size 2 wellies

           soft grass
             in the afternoon
           baby smells in the park

Sweet Spring rain
  on my lips –
the cracks in a wall

Thrush on the ground
    next to the sycamore branch
Still bobbing

                                        Sun breaking through –
                                            flowers glad to see the last
                                        Of winter

the seagulls battle
with the gale
until they agree with it

                                        piñata –
                                            a broken skull
                                        on the wooden table

dove song
    clay pots rattle
on the veranda

empty glasses –
   last night's
inspiration

                              A quiet pint
                                 with Cardiff geezers
                              Sri Lanka win the cricket

On the giant rock
filling up with tears
a young woman stares out into space

                              after fifty years of marriage
                              silence
                              in the hospice

flicking through daydreams
until I find you again –
silent eyes beneath a blue sky

three swallows
   from Africa
a cold Spring evening

                       contrails slice the sky –
                         your blue and white
                       picnic tablecloth

rows of houses
   balance on the hill
the earth is strong

                       you, scratching grass
                         from between the stones
                       – magpies squawk

the hush of bamboo
   soothes
the roar of racing cars

Virginia creeper
  painting rust
on the old grey locomotive

                              Bank holiday –
                                the breeze trying to
                              silence unnecessary cars

We bought a new front door
  to Spring clean
the imagination

                              she tells me her son
                              has escaped to Australia…
                              tea steam rising

I shut the door
your necklace breaks
and beads bounce upon the wooden floor

you throw your green dress
on the oakwood floor –
'OK, kiss me until morning'

                    yellow crocus
                    emerging through snow –
                    a blanket on the baby

a light breeze
disturbs the May blossom
a butterfly survives the destruction

                    smelling your perfume
                    I realise far too slowly
                    I'm smiling
                    at the wrong person

Swifts dive bomb
  the cliff –
Henna on your face

Summer

Pia mater, dura mater
the clouds above my head
a trillion molecules of consciousness

                                    Lopsided pines
                                        point
                                  to the old church

Patterned sky
  b l u e   a n d   w h i t e –
a billion beers worth... if only

                                  A soft day on the senses
                                      Pen y Fan is shrouded
                                  in thick mist

The blazing decking
  you offer me a beer
And return to stir your saucepans

a quiet afternoon
once in a lifetime
- Zanzibar turtle

the frantic hummingbird
tasting sugar
my lovers kiss

Chain gangs of electricity
on the green mountain
armies marching

a pile of books
waiting to build
the mind's hut

moonlight leaks
through summer clouds –
you're leaving

June rain –
  you smile
before leaving

            butterflies
              in the spreading oak tree
            – heart murmurs

My birthday
  you twist the bottle top
Of age

            imprisoned by rain
            our dog died
            last month

White sand in my rucksack
years later
I dream of Africa

shredding love letters
  machine jam
I cut my fingers

                    your smile
                      colour pops my heart
                    red geraniums

sitting seagull
floating on the sea
deep blue sky

                    protruding branch
                    the river still dripping
                    from the kingfisher

elephants remember
  old trails
in your summer garden

Tierra del fuego –
  in the middle of summer
red ice

                              summer street lamps
                              moths get high
                              on a line of moons

Humpbacks breaching
  out of southern seas –
you spray your beer

                              hammock sags in the middle
                              over parched earth –
                              Indian summer

pruning scrubs
  in the middle
of the orange afternoon

yellow grass
all that's left
of lovers' plans

                              Heat haze on paper
                                 sleepy –
                              as cars crawl by

Henley peahens
   strutting at bus stops
old men silent at cafes

                              the burning plastic
                              of garden furniture
                              sticky skin

sipping coffee from Kenya
   in China cups
complaining about immigrants

you refuse to tell me
the whole story
but it's probably enough

                                    giant
                                    beech
                                    trees
                                    stretch
                                    me
                                    to
                                    the
                                    clouds

your house for sale –
   sparrows
picking through the gravel drive

                                    consultant's waiting room
                                    the plant in the window
                                    dead

deep mud tracks
hard to change direction
when you're in fifth gear

I say I'm sorry
without filling in the words –
red eyes

druid circle –
a ghost now
in our wedding photographs

in the small pond
tadpoles dart
upstairs a new bedspread

tracing winter landscapes
your fingers
on my scar tissue

without stopping to pause once
the moss grows back
between the cracks

                              sheets of rain
                              in mid-summer
                              dividing the year

sunshine in the cathedral
through stained glass windows –
old photographers scratch beards

                              Summer hikes
                                 past cairns and lakes
                              – The late drive

your old dream catcher sagging in the middle –
it's OK
it's only cobwebs

my mp3 player
drowning out the sound of birdsong –
my mistake

the forestry workers
drink their tea
woodpecker waits

Sunshine on my face
all evening
Holding a beer

The lofty oaks
of summer
Gently smother me

Frogs hiding
in the reeds
The sky full of diamonds

Lemon twist of sunshine
  ice-cube melts
on brown skin

                    Saltwater decanting
                      from my body
                    Ruby sun

Feathers Hotel, Ludlow
James I room, real ale
no frogs, just silence

                    Brown branch –
                      the result of months
                    in the country sun

straw-hat dusk –
a dog's barking
stretches the day

the first bat
sees the kitchen lights
before we turn them off

puppy breathing
next to me
– waiting for the sun

Lili the dog
discovering the world
a leaf at a time

breaching whales
off the Queensland coast
'oohs and aahs'

the earth bone-dry
under the oak tree –
then heavy summer rain

Oxwich Bay at midnight
red coals amongst the sand
– lapping waves

                              Eve holds a buttercup
                              I break the silence
                              with a smile

watching the rock pool ballroom
Cinderella fish dart for cover
– a trick of the clouds

                              sunlight threads the oaks
                              green and red flashes
                              of woodpecker

reaching the grass seed summit
surveying his kingdom
– the zombie ant

the smiling deaf and dumb couple
sat opposite each other
– noisy pub

growing strong
on love and meat
Lili the dog

the full moon is huge
we walk in the wind of Tenby
crashing through waves of conversations

watching the full moon
move across the sky
still telling stories at dawn

a Lou Reed Saturday
heckling over warm beer
she's only here for a moment

the Zambezi holds a mirror to the sky
– we burn through the dusk

drunk under the oak tree
comfort
with shades of friendship

one mellow evening
both the city church and mosque
offer roosts for rooks

colours in your photograph
have faded in the sun
– love dementia

Sparrowhawk hidden in pine
  everyone else listening
to the sparrow's song

Autumn

rock dimples
  lined with lichen
gather raindrops

                    You're baking bread
                      in the kitchen
                    Swallows swoop outside

toys packed away
in a wooden trunk
falling leaves

                    House empty
                      college calls –
                    You're on your way

Rubble of leaves
the bread in my cupboard
harvests mould

everyone reluctant
to move closer
- coffin lowered

blowing in the breeze
the wooden slats
deep breath in the morning

November 6th
Lonely
as a single star

metal wires
gathering
a harvest of crows

Midday heat
sparrows sing
mellow sleepy head

that brief moment
of togetherness
she lights a cigarette

the evening sun
white –
heading West

after the fireworks
in the Western sky
the night closes in again

my shadow
on your face –
a storm is brewing

orange edge of dusk
sipping white wine
outdoors

rock paper scissors
the game you play
with two men

seasonal floods
over infertile soil –
old age

the better they play
the less rain soaks the hat
buskers

my father's gold ring
hiding in the drawer
– all that's left

cold rain soaks the homeless man
church bells
still ring

divorce papers stuck in the letterbox
the fish are racing each other around the tank
– it's late

by ten o'clock
my mother's ready
frost outside already melted

3am, puppy barking –
I took the battery
from my alarm clock

Wagging your tail
through a field
Of golden grass

scratching off old wallpaper
memories flooding back
one autumn afternoon

Jukebox strugglin' to be heard
over the sound
of singing

                          doing up laces
                          on nanny's shoes
                          the open fire burns my back

clutching her high heels to her breast
an angel limps home
with wet feet

                          raindrops wait patiently
                          on our bedroom window
                          eyes on eyes

walking the length of Main Street
only certain doorways
offer shelter from the storm

how long is too long?
to watch a slimy snail's
marathon across the garden path
in the rain

asleep on her feet
my beautiful dog
until supper time

even though we share
the same fragile sky
our bombs are different colours

my whole magnificent life
shrunk to a single word
on the doctor's lips

sadness in the orchard
counting the rotten fruit
but then a Red Admiral rises…

our daughter's left
for University –
apples falling

a lifelong recession –
  my people good
at building hope

Golden leaves –
not wanting to change
out of my shorts

rusty railings
outside the museum
– prehistoric dinosaurs
dusted daily

strugglin' to make friends
with red bracken
– burnt out car

slow moving river
shopping trolley
gathering rain

                              cobwebs vibrating
                              dewy dawn
                              no sign of the heavy wren

red bladderwrack
on white stony beach
the sea nowhere to be seen

                              third week –
                              trying to buy a beer
                              with old stories

reflected in your Ray Bans
the old broken farm
of your childhood

inside the old pub
bored kids trace
stained glass tattoos

Western moon
fat over endless terraces
watchful eye

The birdsong getting louder
  as the river rages
Copper bracken

a rabbit bolted
hardly heard
above the rush of water

November 12
a lonely soldier
reads words cut in stone

thrushes scampering
  underfoot
light cool rain

                    factory hooter –
                    old men shopping in town
                    gulp

the boy who was going to be an astronaut
packing fruit
before dawn

                    sniffing to herself
                    she fills the vase with water
                    to help dead flowers

blaming Kepler-22b
for all those horrid things you said
stars bright

Winter

modelling the theatre gown
she combs her grey hair
one last time

Raindrops in a puddle
surround your
bright red Wellington boots

your favourite chair by the window
still catches the sun
each early morn

Pulling the string tight
around your neck
North wind

Reflections in the shop window –
ice cream cones
held tight

Seaside cold
  even the gulls
have gone home

hikers hike
dogs sniff ice
one Boxing Day

frost scratching at the window
  tentacles of brambles
wrap around

outrageous sky
grass and tree
a Roman road

not even hot salty tears
can halt the march of winter
cold tea

The puppet master
   closes the curtains
Early on a Saturday

                              Pubs filling up
                                 thick coats removed
                              Warm inside

The girl from the chocolate shop
   crosses the road
To avoid the drunks

                              She's in Abergavenny
                                 as far away
                              as the ocean

Swallowing flies –
the bitter taste
of summers end

blowing wet kisses to the wind
my daughter's t-shirts
on the line

                                my reflection
                                in your blue-grey eyes –
                                ice outside the pub

That nervous smile
  that turns me on
Your blinking eyes

                                awkward chat
                                  floats away
                                on the black water

Frost galvanising the slate
  my lover doing up
buttons on my coat

heads down trudging
   to offices in rain
mice on a wheel
in the pet shop window

                              my co-workers
                              with no magnificence –
                              drizzle

bastards every last one of them
driving home from work
in the rain

                              laughing at the talent
                              the mocking birds
                              – inadequate

so many years
of promises –
swallows fly

rooks swapping branches
beer garden full
of women

Disco lights
  in the nightclub
the black woman's eyes

cold Transvaal night
a warm donkey is killed
by the motorbike

on your shiny wet mouth
the outline
of another's lips

you walked out of the pub
alone –
cold wind blows in

me and her
not speaking –
frost on the windshield

in the eye
of the road-killed fox
headlights shine

black ice –
another makeshift shrine
at the roadside

hearing the drone
of the motorway
– Thunder stopped

watering
your pitcher plant –
Singing *'I'm up to my neck in love…'*

between the snowy branches
floats
the Milky Way

          silently
            watching the lovers
          the city statue

even the scarecrow looks tired
as the Polish workers
leave the icy fields

          leaving the bar
          I'm weighed down
          by your arm

my cousin lowered into the grave
as the workmen down tools –
black crows

the weather turns –
you catch snowflakes
in your bronzed fingers

unsure
above the Cardiff mosque
half moon

Snowflakes sticking
  to your little paws
– your eyes so bright

Your white whiskers
  taking over
The face in time

the empty garden
  in winter –
a robin makes his own path

Shadows advance on smokers
  outside the pub
snow

        Church bells ring
          near rush hour traffic
        calling you back

whale bones
on the deserted beach
winter well and truly here

        'they're a nuisance coming
        and a damn nuisance going
        – teeth'

               Doris Adams

winter night
pausing on each stair –
mother

blackbirds gone now
  snow melting
in footprints

                    A tawny owl
                      screeches a farewell
                    Above a billion stars

knickerless girls
queuing outside the nightclub
cold winter wind

                    Blue-grey hazel
                      black-bud winter
                    Moon-rise

in the gutter now
after too much cider
a slur of drizzle

heads withdrawn
scampering past the accident
snails on speed

puppy dreaming
moves closer to me
the night is black

two cigarettes under one shelter
envying the inside
they huddle closer

If only the street singer
could swap
hailstones for coins

Post-it notes
unread on the fridge
the funeral tomorrow

The bride's father
  alone outside the church
Stamping on the confetti

Pigs squealing
  for as long as they can
– slaughterhouse

folding my childhood
into bed sheets
wind blows my mother's hair

alone in the café
  counting the crumbs
peaceful now

one perfect moon
  your loving face
lights up

Notes

Spring

page 9

Remembering my daughter heading off to school on 1st March, 2007 (St David is the patron saint of Wales). She has a daffodil pinned proudly to her costume but also wanted a flower for her doll, so 'her companion' will look the part and fit in too. I hope a fear of non-conformity hasn't been instilled in her already.

The impetuousness of youth. Thinking how the bluebells flowered too soon this year, before the last frost had gone. The encouraging birds, a youthful party... but the wise old oak knows better.

The starlings dancing between the telephone wires outside our back.

Chinese (Asian) students at the University of Glamorgan surrounded by the large campus trees. The word 'East' refers to their origin, and as students they are youthful and fresh. The words 'Wood' and 'Green' relate to them exploring their new environment and also to the 'Zen' associations with Spring.

page 11

My suburban nightmare, working all week then washing the car, doing the lawn on a Sunday while time 'marches' on.

Young children live only in the present tense. If my daughter knew the sea would wash away her hard work she'd either cry or stay behind and try to rescue them!

Everyone who saw our old dog, Sandy, thought she was so pretty because of her black 'eyeliner' markings. Women (and men) look better when they 'smile' yet many women think that 'make-up' makes them look attractive – this is the contrasting image – a natural beauty versus the artificial.

The 'water untouched' was a sign she was ill.

page 12

When we decided to take Sandy to the vets I carried her to the car and she 'looked up at the moon' and then collapsed and died in my arms.

We can't bear to put away Sandy's toys. We wait for her to come back.

Writing haiku has become cathartic yet I still cry at breakfast time.

Forgetting she's gone and still saying goodbye each morning before leaving for work.

page 13

How grief rises and returns from the most unexpected places at the most unexpected times.

How funny it is walking without a dog. People look at you strange. The 'dew' washes away the grief. Feeling the healing power and utter neutrality of nature.

The silence both inside and outside the house is overpowering without our dog around. You hear every tiny sound.

I even miss the dog's hair I used to curse.

page 14

Without our dog to chase away the cats... 'the blackbird' is fooled into thinking the back yard is safe.

Can't be bothered to do anything, except drink. The *dash* points to 'nothing' because that is all there is. This might also be seen as a dig at the so-called 'academics' who would seek to criticise the form used.

The contrast between waking up late with a hangover and wasting the day, the Monday morning rat-race ever-closer, yet... 'afternoon' drags. Also there is nothing to do on a Sunday where there once was long walks with the dog.

My work shirts seem to come alive and create pictures in the wind as they try to escape into the freedom of the sky, but as they are tied to the 'line' I only feel trapped in my dead-end job.

We go on holiday to Sri Lanka and I think how some people would prefer to read about life rather than live it.

page 15

On holiday in Sri Lanka we visit Dambulla and whilst waiting for the monks to come out of the caves so we can go in and see the Buddhas we sit and watch the frogs jumping into the lily ponds. (c.f. Basho's famous frog poem!)

In Kandy, Sri Lanka the 'sacred relic of the tooth' is a shrine where it is said one of the Buddha's teeth resides. It is a very holy place and the elephants that live in the complex have been trained to stop and bow in front of the temple. Although it is quite contrived and I am not at all religious, to see them do it is still quite moving.

In Swahili the word 'safari' means journey and is one I've used ever since living in Kenya to mean just that. Returning to Wales after our holiday the weather changes and we're back to reality again!

Back from holidays to an empty house, being outdoors still not quite the same without Sandy.

We always seem to miss out on two or three weeks of our mundane life at home when we're overseas as we rarely see a newspaper or TV. The last day before work is often spent quickly catching up on the latest gossip and local news.

page16
Wondering if there was more we could have done for our pet dog?

'Scars' refer to the old adage that time's a great healer. True in many ways but we must also remember that it is 'time' that kills us. The gap before 'time' is to indicate time going on.

The fields are relatively empty of sheep because it's lambing time and with the weather so bad the farmers have taken them indoors.

page 17

A recent fashion amongst local women was to wear a plastic flower in the hair when going out for the night. I'm comparing the arrogant and quite often aggressive attitude that many young girls have to the 'barbed wire' that snares animals. Social commentators are always moaning that young people 'have nothing to do' yet they have TV, iPods, the internet, cinemas, fast food, shops, cars and all manner of organised activities whilst all I had as a teenager was the local library, my old bike and the mountains and streams.

The large puddles over Pontypridd Common seem like oceans to a small child.

Finally the spell of depression begins to break, 'cracks in a wall' like the cracks in dry lips that are slowly healed by the 'Sweet' 'rain' of 'Spring'.

page 18

Sometimes you just have to accept you'll never win by fighting against the status quo.

Eve has a great birthday party, April is hot and we play games over the mountain. Afterwards, back at the house the kids smash homemade balloon piñatas filled with sweets on the decking.

page 19

When the sun is out we sit and drink on the decking. The more beer and wine we consume the more we solve the world's problems.

Drinking in the Old Arcade with 'the Welsh cockneys', watching sport on a Saturday afternoon. Cardiff always used to be such a friendly, multicultural city, although it is losing some of that now with ghettos developing in certain areas. Back from Sri Lanka it's like another lifetime ago and strange to watch the cricket in Wales rather than in Asia.

Near the Rocking Stones on Pontypridd Common is the old 'Cottage Hospital' – now a hospice for dying cancer patients. Throughout the year we often see different people (friends and relatives of the sick) walking near the stones, sometimes sitting, contemplating… then after a few days or weeks we don't see them ever again.

page 20

The patterns in the sky seem like a mirror image of the tablecloth (picnic blanket).

The Welsh 'earth' must be 'strong' to support so many houses, people and cars, all crammed together, tight on sloping mountainsides, especially after the coal mining has taken away much of the earth beneath. And a hint at the spirit holding the people together.

Magpies waiting for anything shiny that may get disturbed as my wife cleans the flagstones out the back.

Boy racers ruining the silence of a holiday. 'Bamboo' plants (nature) dampen the noise / offer respite, a place to hide.

page 21

Using the word 'unnecessary' to ask the question 'why is it that during holidays people seem to be obsessed with spending the day stuck in traffic jams or heading off to DIY stores?' Why can't people just relax and chill out a bit more?

Every important decision is made over a cup of tea…
Greg, my stepson was planning on living in Australia
and our friends in Adelaide were looking for a job for
him. The 'steam rising' can be compared to the aircraft
rising or the son fleeing the nest…

page 22

It seems that couples who have more difficulty
conceiving than others protect ('blanket') their
offspring far more than couples who just seem to churn
them out.

An example of classical conditioning. Sometimes we
catch a familiar scent ('perfume') and it immediately,
and without warning, catapults us back to a time and a
place in the past. It can also get us into trouble.

In Sri Lanka we visited a huge rock (Sygiria) and the
swifts flying around its 'face' were like tiny specks.

Summer

page 25

The structure of the human brain, the trillions of nerve
endings, the possibilities of thought.

Years seem to have flown by while we've been sitting on the decking in the sun, sipping beer and solving the world's problems. Startled by the contrast between the infinite sky and finite life we all have.

page 27

I've just drawn a turtle and played with it in Photoshop. Later I sit on the decking with a beer daydreaming about many years earlier when we watched Hawksbill and Green turtles in Zanzibar, Tanzania. It seems like forever ago and I wonder if we'll ever go back or do anything so wonderful again.

'Hummingbird' - my wife says she doesn't see the point of haiku so I write one from her perspective.

The pylons seem like 'chain gangs' as they 'march' across and ruin our beautiful landscape. I know we need electricity, but do we really need so much of it and couldn't the cables be put underground?

page 28

Many different species of lepidopteron can live in 'oak trees'. An example of the complexity and interaction of nature.

Packing my rucksack for a holiday I notice 'white sand' on the floor and realise it could only have come from Africa - Kenya, Tanzania etc. It takes me back...

page 29

A Photoshop expression - 'colour pops'. Also 'red' is the colour most photographers like to play with.

Migrating elephants will return to the same spot year after year and don't like it when barriers are put in their way. They often get into trouble when they try to tear down fences to continue their journey. People should do well to remember to be 'open' to nature.

page 30

How all animals ('moths' in this case) can become distracted / disorientated by the things in our modern world. Perhaps there is a lesson here for us too?

page 31

After camping out for a few days the grass turns yellow under the tent.

Every year there's a different fashion. Brands like Henley, Hollister etc. are the 'must-be-seen-in' crap clothing. 'Old men' aren't old but experienced (or sensible - take your pick), they just know that it's all transient and utterly unimportant.

I always find it funny listening to 'Daily Mail' readers… whether we are all 'racist' is unclear but one thing we have most definitely done is adopt just about every cultural idea, material, food or artefact we deem useful from our past empire.

page 32
I love to walk through 'beech tree woods' – so uplifting (hence poem structure), you can almost taste the oxygen in the sky!

page 33
On one of the first walks I took on Pontypridd Common I felt a 'ghost' brush past and through me. I jumped a mile even though my wife said not to worry as it was only Dr Price (a famous Welsh character). When we got married we took photographs by the 'druid circle' and in them I can see my father who was dying of cancer at the time. No ghost has ever walked through me again but I often wish one would just so I can ask him if he's OK.

page 34
Taking a camera class down to Llandaf I can't help seeing the resemblance between a bearded Jesus in the 'stained glass windows' and my students. Not long after this was written a friend and member of the class died and so the word 'sunshine' seems even more poignant.

page 35
'My mp3 player' - how often do we get a chance to reconnect with nature yet pass up the chance?

In times of plenty (e.g. summer) animals often get time for a break too.

We are more sensitive to sound at night probably due to there being less ambient noise around. Colder nights also affect how sound travels. The frogs are probably hiding from me rather than the stars though!

page 36
A modern moment on my birthday whilst sat upstairs in the famous Feathers Hotel with a beer. 'No frogs' is a reference to Basho's famous 'frog' haiku.

page 37
The cycles of nature, famine then plenty, drought then flood.

page 38
BBQ on the beach with Warren and gang.

Some moments are just too beautiful for speech.

Several species of ant, from Brazil to Thailand can become infected with a parasitic fungus which causes changes to the ant's brain. These 'zombie' ants alter their behaviour and sometimes climb to the tops of plants where they get eaten and the life cycle continues.

page 39
The pub too noisy to talk but it doesn't bother the deaf and dumb couple. We all forget how lucky we are and so often neglect our other senses.

'Growing strong' – from Basho's vegetarian haiku... Dogs are carnivores of course.

How the moon can influence the tides. A full-on assault of the senses.

A 'Lou Reed Saturday' – playing the jukebox in a local pub, searching for 'Sweet Jane' or 'Rock and Roll'. The moments of drunken completeness are often far too brief.

page 40
Breaking the rules big time – a river can't 'hold a
mirror' but that is what I felt as the slow moving
Zambezi reflected the sky. A precious moment at
Victoria Falls.

The word 'mellow' refers to late summer but I also use
it to ask why Christians and Muslims can't just calm
down and 'get on' a bit better.

How love can fade with time like memories.

Autumn

page 43
We often overlook small things, yet these can also be
beautiful.

How our inertia can cause us to gather depression.
Contrast this time of year with Spring and the cleaning
out of old problems.

page 45
No-one wants to be the first to get closer to death and
no-one wants to be the first one to claim they loved him
the most, in case there's an argument over it later in the
pub. And how silly it is that worrying over these trivial
things can mean we lose a precious moment forever.

The day after bonfire night a single firework seems lost amongst the empty sky.

page 46
Getting too close for comfort or the new art of 'smirting'?

page 47
The older people get the less they have sex. Almost seems to be nature's way of saying 'you've no business trying to reproduce now, you had your chance and you blew it'.

Listening to the town's 'church bells' and thinking of Blake's 'Garden of Love'. Although the church appears to welcome us all, the truly needy seem to be neglected in this day and age just as they have always been.

page 48
Got a new puppy and once she was awake no-one else would sleep.

page 49
Why do girls wear such uncomfortable shoes on a night out? They only end up taking them off.

The journey through life is the same for all peoples of the world but our cultural and religious differences mean we rarely find a common ground.

page 50

We should all try to take time to appreciate nature in our ever-distracting material world. The word 'slimy' is used to highlight the fact that every creature, no matter how ugly, pointless or unpleasant that society deems it, has merit or plays a part in the ecosystem we so readily ignore. The extra 4th line is added on purpose to make the poem last longer instead of just adding an adjective like 'rainy' or 'wet' to the garden path.

A modern version of Basho's blue heron 'enlightenment' poem. These days it seems we are so far removed from nature that we need to define our own idea of 'beautiful'. This was written after a long, tiring afternoon walk and my 11 month old puppy standing so regal, desperate not to fall asleep before her supper arrived when she would once again return to the mortal world.

We all share the same environment, breathe the same air, drink the same water, worship the same sun, yet we still have wars over it

A single word like 'cancer', 'tumour', 'terminal', 'dying' etc. can change a person's whole life in a split second.

Red Admiral butterflies often feed on rotten fruit in autumn and this extra food means they can over winter. The word 'but' refers to the joy we experience when we realise there is something positive to be found in a desperate situation.

page 51

The Welsh nation have always been oppressed by the English government yet the people are still optimistic.

page 52

Taking photographs at 'Cold Knapp, Barry' on a deserted pebble beach in autumn.

After a certain amount of time unemployed the money starts to run out and charity with it.

Years later, walking past the old haunted farm and looking at it ('Ray Bans') in a different light.

page 53

How the sounds of nature compete to be heard.

The day after armistice when the crowds have all gone away I watch an old man run his finger up and down the names on the cenotaph (war monument).

page 54

Trying to coax back to life a broken relationship.

Retired workers collectively frightened by the memory of the 'factory hooter' and all it stood for.

The newly discovered planet, Kepler-22b, in another solar system that could, in theory, hold life. Maybe in an alternative reality things will be different?

Winter

page 57

The hospital is often the last place we see or we're seen in.

Even in winter, and rain we can still find some joy ('bright, red').

Sandy the dog had a 'favourite chair' but so did my father. Guess this is why my mother moved.

When confronted by reality ('reflection') we all hold on tighter to the things we love.

page 59

Our annual trek up Pen y Fan after Christmas.

My Uncle Albert's house. My nan said he was the only man in Cilfynydd who could lie in bed and pick blackberries.

Brecon Beacons - how nature outlives every civilisation.

'Salt' is put on snow and ice to melt it.

page 60

Only those in control ('puppet master') can decide when the fun will end.

The class system on the same street, in the same town and so on... yet those different cultures rarely meet, nor do they wish to.

I find out that an old friend lives in 'Abergavenny'. But even though it's only a forty-five minute drive away it might as well be the other side of the world such are our busy lives now. As we get older we seem to travel less and less, choosing to stay close to our own little patch and our own little lives. Even visits to the city pubs seem to have been abandoned these days.

page 61

An argument inside the pub. The 'frost' grows without a sound.

page 62

Feeling disconnected from the world of work that I've endured for nearly thirty years and yet have nothing to show for it except disappointment.

By the time most people retire they are 'bastards' in the sense their fathers have long since died. But this could be read as 'poor bastards' – all of us!

page 63

Watching the rooks search for a roost from the warmth of a Wetherspoons pub where women also vie for position to be seen by men.

In South Africa the nights can be cold. Wild donkeys (and game) that roam the Northern Transvaal often wander onto the tarmac at night as the road retains the heat better than the surrounding bush. As a result many animals are killed by fast moving vehicles. A good friend of mine once clipped the end of a donkey's nose at approximately 100mph and nearly died himself. The donkey didn't do so well unfortunately. (c.f. Basho's moralistic 'Mukuge' or Hibiscus haiku.)

page 64

I hate 'roadkill' and wish the light from our cars could bring back to life the unfortunate animal. Not sure why 'cats eyes' are being removed from our roads these days either?

Adopted from European countries, in the UK now, we see far too many 'roadside' 'shrines'. Some deaths are caused by accidents of course ('black ice') but many more are caused by idiots.

A 'pitcher plant' is carnivorous – compare this to love... *quote* is from a favourite Robyn Hitchcock song.

page 65
If only statues could talk?

Thinking about some of our Polish friends and how hard they are prepared to work compared to some of our own people.

My cousin Brian's funeral. Even though they've seen it a hundred times before the workmen still pause out of respect yet the crows who inhabit a far harsher world carry on as usual.

page 66
I wrote this poem after looking at the statue of John
Batchelor in Cardiff. He was a Liberal and anti-slavery
campaigner who opposed the Tories. How times
change?

A 'half-moon' (not a crescent moon) highlighting the
fact that the symbol predates Islam by thousands of
years. We should also realise that all celestial bodies
were around many millions of years before the men
who created the different religions came along and
stole them from the pantheists, who surely adopted
them first.

page 67
The words 'Shadows' and 'advance' indicate the silent
creeping (lung shadow) of death (lung cancer) that
many smokers will experience. Winter refers to death
too of course.

Even on a Sunday the traffic is bad as we lose sight of
any kind of spiritual fulfilment. Nowadays we prefer to
worship the god of capitalism at out of town shopping
centres.

A humorous quote from my nan (Doris Adams) –
'teeth'

page 68
Girls these days are not exactly Marilyn Monroe (c.f.
'wind' blowing up dresses).

page 69
A snapshot of the valleys underclass. The winos from
town forget about their crutches and limps (good for a
claim and evidence of unsuitability for work) and move
fast to get out of the way when someone else 'falls' over
the loose paving slabs on Taff Street. Afraid the police
will blame them and interrupt their ritualistic drinking
and drug taking by asking difficult questions.

Wondering which season is the most tactile. Is it winter
when we need hugs to keep warm or is it summer
when we are half naked and hopefully more attractive?

Although I'm as guilty as everyone I'm always amazed
at the amount of trivia ('Post-it notes') we decorate our
lives with.

page 70
Every father's nightmare – his daughter chooses an
unsuitable partner.

When we know the end is near we want more life.

After she leaves the 'café' I'm all 'alone' again with my
thoughts. Replaying all the moments but at peace at last
knowing the relationship has ended.

Some of the poems appearing in this collection have been previously published in the following internationally renowned haiku publications:

Bottlerockets, Presence, Shamrock Haiku Journal, Haiku Quarterly Poetry Magazine, The Heron's Nest

For more information visit Dave's web site:

www.david-lewis.co.uk

MALPAS

20/7/2017